A 31-Day Experiment

Building a Positive Self-image

OTHER BOOKS BY DICK PURNELL

A 31-DAY EXPERIMENT
REVISED & EXPANDED

Building a Positive
SELF IMAGE

DICK PURNELL

THOMAS NELSON PUBLISHERS
Nashville

Published in Nashville, Tennessee, by Thomas Nelson, Inc., Publishers, and distributed in Canada by Word Communications, Ltd., Richmond, British Columbia, and in the United Kingdom by Word (UK), Ltd., Milton Keynes, England.

Scripture quotations are taken from the HOLY BIBLE, NEW INTERNATIONAL VERSION ®. Copyright © 1973, 1978, 1984 by International Bible Society. Used by permission of Zondervan Bible Publishing House. All rights reserved.

The "NIV" and "New International Version" trademarks are registered in the United States Patent and Trademark Office by International Bible Society. Use of either trademark requires the permission of International Bible Society.

Library of Congress Cataloging-in-Publication Data

Purnell, Dick.
  Building a positive self-image : a 31-day experiment / Dick Purnell. — Rev. & expanded.
      p.   cm
   Originally published: San Bernardino, CA : Here's Life Publishers © 1990.
   Includes bibliographical references.
   ISBN 0-8407-6948-2 (pbk.)
   1. Self-perception—Religious aspects—Christianity.
2. Devotional exercises. I. Title.
BV4598.25.P87 1993
248.4—dc20
                                                    92-44461
                                                        CIP

Printed in the United States of America
1 2 3 4 5 6 7 - 99 98 97 96 95 94 93

**To Bill Bright
(President of Campus Crusade for Christ)**

For the past 30 years

you have inspired me to

biblical thinking and godly living

CONTENTS

▼▼▼

YOU + GOD = A GREAT COMBINATION

I remember seeing a famous movie star being interviewed on TV. As he answered a number of questions about his life, he mentioned he was seeing a psychiatrist and struggling with some things that troubled him.

The interviewer asked an astute question, "When you walk down the streets of New York, or any other big city, and see your name up there on the marquee in lights, what do you think about?"

The actor thought for a minute and then replied, "When I see my name in lights I think to myself, *Someday I would like to meet that man.*"

He was saying there is a big difference between the image the public saw of him—flashy, successful, happy-go-lucky, and famous—and the real person, that below-the-surface part of him that was unsure and struggling to somehow get his life in order.

Have you ever felt like there were two people inside you? One is the outside person everybody talks to, says "hello" to, and interacts with. The other is the "deep-down inside" you—the one hardly anybody ever hears from or sees, the one only you really know. We are often afraid to let this inner person out because we have a hard time liking that part of ourselves. Sometimes we feel inadequate and self-conscious.

What are your thoughts and feelings about your "deep-down inside" self? Do you sometimes feel discouraged and want to give up? You experience ups and downs that increase your desire for stability, strength, and understanding. The school of hard knocks has made your self-esteem black and blue, and you are wondering if there is a way to get on the positive side.

You are not alone. The Bible is full of people who felt the same way. Moses had painful questions about himself. In Exodus 3:4, when Moses was an eighty-year-old shepherd, he was confronted by God in a burning bush. God called out saying, "Moses, Moses," and Moses responded by saying, "Here I am." He was confident in being a shepherd and felt self-assured.

But later Moses responded in quite a different way. God told him to go back to Egypt, where he grew up, and to lead His people out from the bondage they were experiencing. God was going to pour all His power, all His joy, all His goodness through Moses and out onto His people to set them free. However, Moses responded this time by asking, "Who am I, that I should go to Pharaoh and bring the Israelites out of Egypt?" (Exodus 3:11).

Moses felt secure in his shepherd duties. But outside of his comfort zone his self-perception was so low he couldn't see what God saw. "Who am I?" was all he could let out. He looked at himself as being fearful and weak and having major inadequacies in his life. He thought he was right by saying, "Who am I? I just can't do it. There's no way, God." Obviously, God was not looking at the facts from Moses' point of view. God saw things from the reality which He knew to be true.

Moses eventually trusted God to strengthen him. God and Moses made a great combination as they led a whole nation out of slavery to become a mighty army ready to conquer the Promised Land.

Have you ever tried to counsel God? "Well,

You have the wrong person, God. You need somebody else. What You are asking me is out of line with who I am."

Yet who are you, really? That's the major question. God wants to do something significant in your life, and it all starts with His coming to you and saying, "I want to fill your life with Myself."

Biblical Thinking

Once I sat in a metal chair on a lawn high in the mountains, looking out over a valley spread out before me. I was impressed with the gleaming buildings and beautiful trees of the city in the distance. As I sat there looking around and taking it all in, I happened to notice a tiny ant climbing up a blade of grass near me. It would get up to the top of the blade with its antennae going all different directions, trying to see out beyond—but it couldn't. So the ant went back down the blade of grass he was on and climbed to the top of another blade of grass. But all he could see was just a bit beyond. And here I sat looking down at him and seeing also this magnificent scene of the mountains and the valley and the city below. I thought, *How much this is like God and me. I can see only a little bit,*

my perception is so limited—but God sees it all.
His perception is so much broader!

You might say that God's perception is "real" reality. It's not what we see that is true, but what He sees. What God has done for us is so significant that we need to look at who we are in His eyes. Our worth as an individual is built on what God has said about us—and His perception about us is the truth.

We often believe that our self-perception is reality. We want to stay in our comfort zone and do only what we believe we can handle, and we often focus on our inadequacies. The message of our world is to be preoccupied with self. But God's way is for us to be preoccupied with biblical thinking and godly living.

God has a specific purpose for each of us and we can trust His purpose and God Himself to be right. His desire for us is that we become all He wants us to be. As we trust Him for it, He will work in us to accomplish His purpose. Four different times the Bible says: "The righteous shall live by faith" (Habakkuk 2:4; Romans 1:17; Galations 3:11; Hebrews 10:38).

God wants to strengthen the "deep-down inside" you! What method does He use? It doesn't come by focusing on self and our weaknesses, but by focusing on His adequacy, on all that He has given to us in order to become what He wants us to be. Biblical thinking is what God says is true, not what we say is true. It is the work of God, helping us to see the "big picture" which He has laid out.

Seeing self as our only resource is wrong thinking. Biblical thinking is to find out what God has said about us and to find His resources for us to live a life of significance, so that the two people in our life—the outside image and the "deep-down inside" us—will be in harmony and have purpose, meaning, and direction.

The apostle Paul had a similar experience like Moses. He had a total change when the Lord revolutionized his life. Here is his testimony:

"I thank Christ Jesus our Lord, who has given me strength, that he considered me faithful, appointing me to his service. Even though I was once a blasphemer and a persecutor and a violent man, I was shown mercy because I acted in ignorance and unbelief. The grace of our Lord was poured out on me abundantly, along with the faith and love that are in Christ Jesus.

"Here is a trustworthy saying that deserves full acceptance: Christ Jesus came into the world to save sinners—of whom I am the worst.

But for that very reason I was shown mercy so that in me, the worst of sinners, Christ Jesus might display his unlimited patience as an example for those who would believe on him and receive eternal life" (1 Timothy 1:12–16).

Biblical thinking is learning to find out exactly what God has said that is true and what reality is in Him. It is finding our security in what He has said, and not what our friends, parents, or the world has to say about us.

Godly Living

The end result will be not just thinking correctly, but living correctly. Godly living is looking at the facts of the Bible, what God has said about us, and then putting these things into practice in our lives. It is based upon biblical thinking.

"So then, just as you received Christ Jesus as Lord, continue to live in him, rooted and built up in him, strengthened in the faith as you were taught, and overflowing with thankfulness" (Colossians 2:6–7).

The Experiment

Do you want to see improvement in your deep-down, personal life? Do you want to grow in your understanding of biblical thinking? Would you like to have godly living as your lifestyle? Then try this *31-Day Experiment: Building a Positive Self-image.*

Examine how you look at yourself and how you live. For one month make a diligent effort to build your confidence and trust in God. Take His view of you as the right view. In Christ you will find acceptance and fulfillment, and the joy and power to live the quality of life that only He can give. You can experience godly living, which is filled with joy and purpose, even in the middle of problems and significant troubles. A positive self-image does not focus on pride or self. Instead, it focuses on God's gifts to you and the adequacy He gives to live life to the fullest.

For the next 31 days let God draw you into His confidence as you work through this Experiment. Let the Scriptures come alive as you begin to understand from God's point of view what He is like and what He has done for you. Then allow those facts to come into play in your life, so that the "deep-down inside" you is strengthened and empowered. You'll begin to really live out all you can be—not in your strength, but in God's strength.

DEVELOPING A BIBLICAL SELF-IMAGE

Here are 31 things you can do toward developing a biblical self-image. These statements are the titles of the passages you will study in this Experiment.

1. Praise the Lord for who He is.

2. Recognize who really knows you.

3. Meditate on the Scriptures.

4. Delight in biblical commandments.

5. Listen to wisdom.

6. Remember God's actions.

7. Look at divine grace.

8. Count yourself alive to God.

9. Become a slave to righteousness.

10. Trust Christ for victory.

11. Depend on the Spirit.

12. Conquer difficulties.

13. Thank the Lord for what He has done.

14. Follow the right leader.

15. Choose to be totally committed.

16. Invest your life wisely.

17. Give generously to needy people.

18. Lead by serving.

19. Seek godly values.

20. Number your days.

21. Stop complaining about your weaknesses.

22. Learn to be truly happy.

23. Renew your mind.

24. Build up the Body of Christ.

25. Know your place in the Body.

26. Love like Christ loves.

27. Improve yourself.

28. Rejoice in difficulties.

29. Live in harmony with other people.

30. Build a precious heritage.

31. Focus on your ultimate future.

MY PRAYER

Dear Lord Jesus Christ,

I am so needy of Your input in my life. As I look into myself, I find an insecure person wanting Your strength and peace.

People don't really know me. My "deep-down inside" person wants to improve. Sometimes I feel insecure, and often I don't even know myself. Only You know the real me. You know me infinitely and perfectly.

My life is in Your hands. My heart is open to You. Pour into me Your peace, love, and strength. Build me up in Your matchless grace and goodness.

As I begin this Experiment, develop in me the kind of self-image that pleases You in all respects. Remove selfishness and pride from me. I want to become all that You want me to be.

Thank You for hearing my prayer.

Signed_____

MY COVENANT WITH GOD

I commit myself before God to do this *Experiment in Building a Positive Self-image* for the next 31 days. Today, I make a covenant with the Lord Jesus to:

1. Spend up to 30 minutes each day in Bible study, prayer, and writing out my thoughts and plans.

2. Ask at least one other Christian to pray daily for me that the Experiment will help me grow in faith (that person may want to do the Experiment along with me so we can share together what we are learning).

3. Attend a church each week where the Word of God is taught.

Signed_____

Date _____

GUIDELINES FOR GROWTH

A. PREPARATION FOR EACH DAY

1. *Equipment.* Have a Bible and pen to record your thoughts and plans in this book.

2. *Time.* Choose a specific half-hour each day to spend with the Lord. Pick the time of day that is best for you—when your heart is most receptive to meeting with God.

3. *Place.* Find a particular spot where you can clear your mind of distractions and focus your full attention on God's Word. Suggestions: bedroom, office, library, living room, lounge, outdoors.

B. READ—20 Minutes

1. Pray earnestly before you begin. Ask the Lord to teach you what He desires you to learn.

2. Read the entire passage.

3. Read it again, looking for important ideas.
4. Make written notes on the following:
    a. Sections A and B—Study the passage thoroughly to answer the questions. Observe what God says about Himself and how people can live dynamic, godly lives. As you discover more of His truth, your understanding of God's purposes for you will increase.
    b. Section C—Decide how you will apply the teachings in the passage.
5. Choose a verse that is especially meaningful to you. Copy it onto a card and read it several times during the day. Think about its meaning and impact on your life. Memorize it when you have free mental time, for example, when you are getting ready in the morning, while you are standing in line, taking a coffee break, waiting for class to begin, or walking somewhere.

C. NEED—5 Minutes
1. Choose what is your most pressing personal need of the day.
2. Write down your request. The more spe-

cific you are, the more specific the answer will be.

3. Earnestly pray each day for God's provision.

4. When the Lord meets your need, record the date and how He did it. Periodically review God's wonderful provisions, and thank Him often for His faithfulness. This will greatly increase your faith.

5. At the end of the month, review all the answers to your prayers. Rejoice in God's goodness to you. Keep praying for the requests that still need answers.

D. DEED—5 Minutes

1. Pray for God's guidance to help another person during the day. Try to apply the particular passage you have just studied.

2. Take the initiative to express God's wonderful love to someone. Be a servant. Someone has said, "Behind every face there is a drama going on." Tap into at least one person's drama.

3. As you help a needy person, tell him (or her) about your faith in Christ. Here are some suggestions for helping:

a. Provide a meal.
b. Take care of his/her children.
c. Help him/her study for a school subject.
d. Do yard work.
e. Write an encouraging letter.
f. Start a Bible study.
g. Teach a sports activity or a mechanical skill.
h. Fix something.
i. Show interest in his/her interests.
j. Give an honest compliment.
k. Pray with him about his or her need.

4. Later, record the details of how the Holy Spirit used you this day. This will increase your confidence to reach out to others. Thank the Lord Jesus for expressing His love and compassion to others through you.

E. APPLICATION

1. Write down ideas about how you would put into practice specific lessons found in the passage.
2. Devise a plan to implement your ideas.

F. LAST THING IN THE EVENING
1. **READ** the passage again, looking for additional facts about God and about His ideas for your developing a positive self-image.
2. Pray again for your **NEED**. Thank the Lord that He will answer in His way and in His time.
3. Record the **DEED** God guided you to accomplish.
4. Review the **APPLICATION** you chose for the day. Did you do it? What did you learn?

G. PARTNERS
Ask a friend or a group of friends to do the Experiment together with you. Pray frequently for one another that you will learn more about the Lord Jesus and how to build a positive self-image. Encourage one another to be disciplined and faithful in completing the Experiment. Share what you are learning.

STARTING POINT— EVALUATION #1

Before beginning this *Experiment in Building a Positive Self-image,* take a few moments to evaluate your life. How do you feel about your relationship with the Lord? How do you feel about yourself?

In order to see measurable progress in building a positive self-image, decide what you want to see accomplished in the next 31 days. Specifically, how would you like to see God develop your self-image? What do you want Him to do in your life?

Change may occur quickly. However, it may take a longer period of time—possibly a month, six months, a year, or more. It is conceivable to take three steps forward and then one step backward, but keep moving. Progress can be made. Each small step of growth is success.

A. SOMETHING TO CHANGE

Choose one attitude or habit you would like to see changed. Here are some suggested areas to work on:

1. A bad attitude that displeases God.

2. Conduct that upsets other people.

3. Temptation that you give in to often.

4. A habit that you know is wrong.

5. Temper that is hard to control.

6. A feeling of failure that depresses you.

I would like to see changed:	This is how, by faith, I will trust God to change it:
LACK OF TIME W/ CHRIST	CREATE URGANCY IN ME

B. SOMETHING TO ACCOMPLISH

What would you like to achieve? Here are some suggestions:

1. Overcome a personality conflict with some-one.

2. Set a good example for someone.

3. Tell a friend about Christ.

4. Start a small-group Bible study.

5. Develop a consistent, daily devotional time with God.

6. Change a weakness into a strength.

I would like to achieve:	This is how, by faith, I will trust God to accomplish it:
BE ATTRACTIVE TO OTHERS in A WAY THAT LEADS TO m'ment	GIVE SENSE OF SERVICE

C. SOMETHING TO HANDLE

Pick an area in your life that you have a difficult time dealing with. Here are some situations you may need to get victory over:

1. Feeling of rejection by someone you care for.

2. Financial pressure that has you worried.

3. A physical ailment which makes you fearful.

4. Loneliness.

5. A specific weakness that bothers you.

6. Something about your looks.

I would like to overcome:	This is how, by faith, I will trust God to handle it:
WEIGHT	CHANGE my LIFESTYLE
EM	WISDOM

THE EXPERIMENT

31 Days

of

Building a Positive Self-Image

Section 1
Biblical Thinking
Days 1–13

PRAISE THE LORD FOR WHO HE IS

Psalm 145:1–21

▼

KEY VERSES:

The LORD is righteous in all his ways and loving toward all he has made. The LORD is near to all who call on him, to all who call on him in truth. He fulfills the desires of those who fear him; he hears their cry and saves them (Psalm 145:17–19).

CRY FOR WHAT
WHAT DOES SAVE MEAN?
FROM WHAT?

TODAY'S FOCUS:

What is God really like? People have many different opinions. The truth is what God has revealed about Himself in the Bible. He is worthy of praise and worship.

READ:

Pray for a responsive heart.

DAY 1

A. Focus on God's character. For what can you praise Him?

- CONSISTENCY
- WANTS ME
- FORGIVING

B. Focus on God's works (His actions). For what can you praise Him?

C. God has affected my life tremendously. I praise Him for:

- GIVING ME A MINISTRY
  OPPORTUNITY

- GROWTH IN FRAN
- CLOSER RELATIONSHIP

32

DAY 1

NEED:

Thank the Lord that He satisfies your desires in His time and His way.

My greatest need today is:

- *TIME WITH HIM*
- *CREATIVITY*
- *GUIDANCE FROM HIM*

God answered my prayers today _____ (date) in this way: *STILL PRAYING*

DEED:

Pray for opportunities to tell others about the Lord's greatness.

O God my King, I will commend Your works to another generation by:

- *OPEN HEART TO HIS LEAD.*
   OF E/M.
- *SEE PRISONER*

▲

APPLICATION:

Write down some of the wonderful things the Lord has done in your life. Take time to praise Him for each one.

RECOGNIZE WHO REALLY KNOWS YOU

Psalm 139:1–24

▼

KEY VERSES:

O Lord, you have searched me and you know me. You know when I sit and when I rise; you perceive my thoughts from afar (Psalm 139:1–2).

TODAY'S FOCUS:

Your "deep-down inside" you is not hidden from the Lord. He knows you! And the wonderful truth is that He understands everything about you and loves you.

READ:

Praise the Lord that He knows all about you.

DAY 2

A. What specifically does the Lord know about
   you? *THOUGHTS, MOTIVES*

B. What has the Lord done for you?
   CREATED ME
   SET MY PATH

C. Since the Lord knows me so well, I:
   CAN TRUST HIM

DAY 2

NEED:

Thank God for His understanding of your "deep-down inside" personal self.

My greatest need today is:

TIME w/HIM
FAITH, SIGN HE is in CONTROL
MOMENTUM.
CLOSE TO HIM

God answered my prayers today _____ (date) in this way:

11-09 STILL PRAYING

DEED:

Pray for God to lead you in the way everlasting.

I pray for specific people that they will:

▲

APPLICATION:

Write down some of the things that only God understands about you. Thank Him for each of these.

WHAT I WANT I DO NOT DO.

MEDITATE ON THE SCRIPTURES

Psalm 119:97–112

▼

KEY VERSES:
Oh, how I love your law! I meditate on it all day
long. Your commands make me wiser than my
enemies, for they are ever with me. I have more
insight than all my teachers, for I meditate on
your statutes (Psalm 119:97–99).

TODAY'S FOCUS:
God's Word gives you direction and wisdom. It
is invaluable to your life.

READ:
Pray for a love for the Scriptures.

DAY 3

A. Describe the psalmist's attitudes about the Bible.

SEAT OF WISDOM — BENEFICIAL

B. What does the Word of God do for a person who lives by it?

*MAKES WISER THAN
OTHERS
LIGHTS PATH*

C. I want to study the Bible because:

GOD TALKS TO ME

DAY 3

NEED:

Praise God that His promises are sweet.

My greatest need today is:

> *DEVOTION TO GOD*
> *DIE TO SELF*

God answered my prayers today _____(date)
in this way:

DEED:

Pray that you will not stray from His precepts.

O Lord, guide me to share Your Word with others today. Here are some ideas that will help me do that:

> *PRISON w/GEORGE*

▲

APPLICATION:

Reread the passage and write down the one action of the psalmist which you most want to emulate. What is your plan for doing that?

DELIGHT IN BIBLICAL COMMANDMENTS

Psalm 119:129–144

▼

KEY VERSES:
You righteousness is everlasting and your law
is true. Trouble and distress have come upon
me, but your commands are my delight. Your
statutes are forever right; give me understanding that I may live (Psalm 119:142–144).

TODAY'S FOCUS:
Your attitude toward God's Word is of utmost
importance. Focus your time on assessing your
attitude and growing in love with God through
His Word.

READ:
Pray for God to teach you His ways.

DAY 4

A.   Describe the characteristics of God's Word.

- GIVES UNDERSTANDING

- FOREVER RIGHT

B.   What does God's Word do for those who obey it?

C.   My attitude toward God's commands is:

WANT TO - DONT DO

NEED PEACE AND UNDERSTANDING

DAY 4

NEED:
Thank God His Word is forever right.

My greatest need today is:

Closoness To H/S.

God answered my prayers today _____(date)
in this way:

DEED:
Pray for understanding as to how to live a godly
life.

Dear Lord, help me communicate Your
Word to:

CHris Mowe

▲

APPLICATION:
God's "promises have been thoroughly tested."
Write down some of God's promises to you and
how they have been proven true in your life.

LISTEN TO WISDOM

Proverbs 8:1–36

▼

KEY VERSES:
Choose my instruction instead of silver, knowledge rather than choice gold, for wisdom is more precious than rubies, and nothing you desire can compare with her (Proverbs 8:10–11).

TODAY'S FOCUS:
The Lord's wisdom cries out, beckoning all to embrace her. In today's confusing world, one of the greatest needs is for godly wisdom.

READ:
Pray to find wisdom and receive favor from the Lord.

A. Why is godly wisdom so desirable?

IT LEADS TO HIM

B. What are some characteristics of a person who has wisdom?

UNDERSTAND

CALM

DONT worry

confident

C. Instead of being concerned about obtaining wealth and possessions, I will concentrate on:

HEARING HIS WISDOM

OBEYING WISDOM

NEED:
Thank the Lord He is the source of wisdom.
    My greatest need today is:

    DISCIPLINE

    God answered my prayers today _____
(date) in this way:

DEED:
Praise God that His wisdom is more precious
than riches.
    Dear Father, help me share godly wisdom
with:

▲

APPLICATION:
Write down areas of your life in which you need
wisdom. Ask God to give you wisdom for each of
these and believe that He will answer.

    MONEY - GIVING
    HOW TO SACRIFICE

REMEMBER GOD'S ACTIONS

Deuteronomy 7:1–26

▼

KEY VERSE:

Know therefore that the LORD your God is God; he is the faithful God, keeping his covenant of love to a thousand generations of those who love him and keep his commands (Deuteronomy 7:9).

TODAY'S FOCUS:

God promised to deliver the Hebrews and so uphold His covenant of love with them. Because He loves you, the promise of deliverance is yours as well!

READ:

Pray for deliverance from difficult problems.

DAY 6

A. Just before God brought the Hebrews into the Promised Land, He promised them He would do great things for them. What were the people supposed to do to receive God's blessing?

obey

B. When the people obeyed God, He would:

bless them

C. When I face difficult circumstances, I will remember that God:

have around me trust to do what he tells me to

NEED:

Thank God for His covenant of love and mighty hand in your life.

My greatest need today is:

FREEDOM FROM SIN

courage to see Trilby

God answered my prayers today _____(date) in this way:

DEED:

Pray for courage to follow God's commands.

Oh, Lord, my God, use me to:

▲

APPLICATION:

Make a list of the events in your life in which the Lord did great things for you. Spend time praising God for His loving faithfulness.

LOOK AT DIVINE GRACE

Romans 5:1–11

▼

KEY VERSES:
Therefore, since we have been justified through
faith, we have peace with God through our Lord
Jesus Christ, through whom we have gained
access by faith into this grace in which we now
stand. And we rejoice in the hope of the glory of
God (Romans 5:1–2).

TODAY'S FOCUS:
You are at peace with God! His divine grace
reconciled you to Himself. He has saved you to
become all He wants you to be.

READ:
Thank God you have peace with Him.

DAY 7

A. What has God done for you?

FORGIVEN ME.

HAS GIVEN PROMISE OF
GROWTH AND IMPROVED
CHARACTER

B. How should you handle suffering and troubles?

- THANK GOD
- ASK GOD TO SHOW REASON.
- REPENT. SUBMIT.
- WITH FAITH IN HIM

C. I know God loves me because:

HE DIED FOR ME, A SINNER

NEED:

Thank Christ for His death and resurrection for you.

My greatest need today is:
MORE DISCIPLINE
DAILY QUIET TIME

- Guy Frank
- Glenn Riley.
- Payton/Primeaux
- Rensburg
- Teachers
- Mission Stint

God answered my prayers today _____
(date) in this way: Bought Riley a Bible
Rensburg @ 5th Event

DEED:

Thank God for reconciliation with Him.

Dear God, pour out Your love through me to:

▲

APPLICATION:

Use a Bible dictionary or commentary to write out definitions of the key words in this passage, such as *justify, faith, grace, hope, glory, saved, reconciliation.* Which word is most meaningful to you? Why?

COUNT YOURSELF ALIVE TO GOD

Romans 6:1–14

▼

KEY VERSES:
In the same way, count yourselves dead to sin but alive to God in Christ Jesus. Therefore do not let sin reign in your mortal body so that you obey its evil desires (Romans 6:11–12).

TODAY'S FOCUS:
Through Christ's powerful resurrection from the dead, you are made alive. This same power is at work in you, giving you strength to live a new life.

READ:
Pray to offer yourself to God.

A. What has happened to you because of Christ's crucifixion?

HAVE A LIFE EMPOWERED
BY HIM, NOT BY FAILURE

TO OBEY THE LAW

SIN'S HOLD WAS GONE

B. What has happened to you because of Christ's resurrection?

ABOVE

C. I will consider myself:

NEEDING FORGIVENESS

OBEDIENT TO CHRIST, NOT LAW.

STANDING ON CHRIST'S
FORGIVENESS, NOT STATURE
REGARDING THE LAW.

DAY 8

NEED:

Thank God for your death to sin and your new life in Christ.

My greatest need today is:

EMPOW OF HOLY SPIRIT
SEE GOD work in FOLLOW UP

God answered my prayers today _____ (date) in this way:

DEED:

Pray that you will be an instrument of righteousness.

Father, guide me to help rescue someone from:

▲

APPLICATION:

What specific attitudes or actions do you want to change? What steps should you take to make those changes?

BECOME A SLAVE TO RIGHTEOUSNESS

Romans 6:15–7:6

▼

KEY VERSES:
But thanks be to God that, though you used to be slaves to sin, you wholeheartedly obeyed the form of teaching to which you were entrusted. You have been set free from sin and have become slaves to righteousness (Romans 6:17–18).

TODAY'S FOCUS:
You have a choice—to become a slave to sin, which leads to death, or a slave to God, which leads to eternal life. Living for God will give you a positive outlook on yourself.

READ:
Pray for understanding.

A. When you became a Christian, you were set free from sin and the law. Why is that important to know?

BECAUSE TEMPTATION STILL EXIST.

B. What are the personal benefits of being enslaved to righteousness?

SELF ESTEEM

C. Because I have been set free from sin and the law, I will:

NEED:
Thank God you have eternal life.
   My greatest need today is:

   God answered my prayers today _____
(date) in this way:

DEED:
Pray to serve in the new way of the Spirit.
   Lord Jesus, show me how to help others
become free from bondage to sin. Give me courage to: *TRUST H/S — not my WORDS*

▲

APPLICATION:
Contrast the results in your life when you were
a slave to sin and when you live like a slave to
righteousness. Which lifestyle do you prefer?

TRUST CHRIST FOR VICTORY

Romans 7:7–25

▼

KEY VERSES:

For in my inner being I delight in God's law; but I see another law at work in the members of my body, waging war against the law of my mind and making me a prisoner of the law of sin at work within my members. What a wretched man I am! Who will rescue me from this body of death? Thanks be to God—through Jesus Christ our Lord! (Romans 7:22–25)

TODAY'S FOCUS:

God's law is good. But your sinful nature rebels against it. Only Christ can solve the problem and give you success in doing what is right.

READ:

Pray for insight.

A. Why do we struggle with doing sinful things that we don't really want to do? What is causing this struggle?

B. How can you get victory over the internal war?

C. Through Christ I am dead to the law. Therefore, I will trust Christ to:

NEED:
Thank God for the freedom Christ gives.
My greatest need today is:

God answered my prayers today _____
(date) in this way:

DEED:
Pray for strength to live victoriously.
Dear God, I want You to free me to:

▲

APPLICATION:
Read a Bible commentary on Romans 7 that
explains the victory you can have over sin in
your life. Write down areas you struggle with.
Trust Christ for victory.

DEPEND ON THE SPIRIT
Romans 8:1–17

▼

KEY VERSES:
Therefore, there is now no condemnation for
those who are in Christ Jesus, because through
Christ Jesus the law of the Spirit of life set me
free from the law of sin and death (Romans
8:1–2).

TODAY'S FOCUS:
When the Spirit of God controls you, He gives
life and peace. He will lead you and assure you
that you are God's child. The Holy Spirit is the
source of power to live in a manner that pleases
God and yourself.

READ:
Pray that you will be controlled by the Spirit.

DAY 11

A. What are the differences between a person living according to the sinful nature and a person living according to the Spirit?

B. If you are a Christian, the Spirit of God lives in you. What does He do for you?

C. I am determined that my mind will be controlled by the Holy Spirit because:

NEED:
Thank God for His provisions for a dynamic life.
My greatest need today is:

God answered my prayer today _____
(date) in this way:

DEED:
Pray for others to become children of God.
Spirit of God, lead me to:

▲

APPLICATION:
List the reasons why you know you are a child
of God.

CONQUER DIFFICULTIES

Romans 8:18–39

▼

KEY VERSES:
No, in all these things we are more than conquerors through him who loved us. For I am convinced that neither death nor life, neither angels nor demons, neither the present nor the future, nor any powers, neither height nor depth, nor anything else in all creation, will be able to separate us from the love of God that is in Christ Jesus our Lord (Romans 8:37–39).

TODAY'S FOCUS:
Though sufferings and troubles are a part of your life, you are assured of God's faithful love for you. The Spirit helps you in your weaknesses so that you will be victorious. Even in the darkest times, you are never alone!

READ:
Thank God that the Holy Spirit intercedes for you.

A. Suffering and weaknesses are not pleasant, but what does God say is the way to handle them?

B. What has the Lord promised you?

C. I have hope that God will:

NEED:
Thank God that nothing can separate you from His love.

My greatest need today is:

God answered my prayers today _____
(date) in this way:

DEED:
Pray for others to be assured of God's love for them.

Jesus Christ, I want to help others to:

▲

APPLICATION:
Describe a time when you doubted God loved you. Did any good (verse 28) come from that time? Explain.

THANK THE LORD FOR WHAT HE HAS DONE

Psalm 103:1–22

▼

KEY VERSES:
Praise the LORD, O my soul; all my inmost being, praise his holy name. Praise the LORD, O my soul, and forget not all his benefits (Psalm 103:1–2).

TODAY'S FOCUS:
As you meditate on all the things the Lord has done for you, praise will fill your heart. Worship will change your focus from self-centered to God-centered.

READ:
Pray for a grateful attitude.

A. No matter what your circumstances are like, you can sing praises to the Lord for His goodness. What can you thank Him for?

B. What are the characteristics of the Lord as found in this psalm?

C. My heart overflows with praise to the Lord because:

NEED:
Thank God for His great works.
    My greatest need today is:

    God answered my prayers today _____
(date) in this way:

DEED:
Praise the Lord that He satisfies your desires
with good things.
    I want someone else to know that the Lord
is:

▲

APPLICATION:
Compose a poem, song, or letter that describes
the goodness of the Lord in your life and in the
world.

THE EXPERIMENT

31 Days

of

Building a Positive Self-Image

Section 2
Godly Living
Days 14–31

FOLLOW THE RIGHT LEADER

John 10:1–30

▼

KEY VERSES:
The thief comes only to steal and kill and destroy; I have come that they may have life, and have it to the full. I am the good shepherd. The good shepherd lays down his life for the sheep (John 10:10–11).

TODAY'S FOCUS:
Jesus describes Himself as the Good Shepherd. He knows you. As you follow Him, your life will be full.

READ:
Pray for your relationship with the Good Shepherd.

A. What does Christ do for His sheep?

B. How do His sheep respond to Him?

C. I know I am one of His sheep for the following reasons:

NEED:
Thank Jesus for holding you in His hand.
My greatest need today is:

God answered my prayers today _____
(date) in this way:

DEED:
Pray for Christ's leading.
Good Shepherd, I am listening to Your voice.
Lead me to:

▲

APPLICATION:
Look up *sheep* in an encyclopedia. In what ways
are you like a sheep? How do you feel about
being like a sheep?

CHOOSE TO BE TOTALLY COMMITTED

Luke 14:15–35

▼

KEY VERSE:

In the same way, any of you who does not give up everything he has cannot be my disciple (Luke 14:33).

TODAY'S FOCUS:

There is a high cost for following Christ. A relationship with Him is more important than anything else. To sacrifice all for Christ is a decision you will never regret.

READ:

Pray for the confidence to give up everything for Christ.

A. Why do some people miss the joy of becoming a disciple of Christ?

B. How can a person become His disciple?

C. My response to Christ's invitation to follow Him is:

NEED:

Thank Christ for His kind invitation to be His follower.

My greatest need today is:

God answered my prayers today _____ (date) in this way:

DEED:

Pray for resolve to count the cost of discipleship.

Master, lead me to people that I can invite to:

▲

APPLICATION:

Divide a sheet of paper in half by drawing a vertical line down the center. On the left side put all the things that could hinder your becoming His disciple. On the other side write down the ways you will overcome those hindrances.

INVEST YOUR LIFE WISELY

Matthew 25:14–30

▼

KEY VERSE:
His master replied, "Well done, good and faithful servant! You have been faithful with a few things; I will put you in charge of many things. Come and share your master's happiness!" (Matthew 25:23)

TODAY'S FOCUS:
Each of us has only one life. What we do now will have a profound result in this world and in the one to come. The greatest goal in life is to please our Master.

READ:
Pray for faithfulness.

A. Why was the Master pleased with the servants who had five and two talents?

B. Why was the Master upset with the servant who had one talent?

C. With all that God has given to me, I will:

NEED:
Thank God for His generosity in giving you gifts.
My greatest need today is:

God answered my prayers today _____
(date) in this way:

DEED:
Pray that you may share the Master's happiness.
Master, I am your servant. Help me to be faithful to:

▲

APPLICATION:
List areas of your life where God has blessed you. Ask Him to guide you to invest them wisely for His glory. Strive to be faithful.

GIVE GENEROUSLY TO NEEDY PEOPLE

Matthew 25:31–46

▼

KEY VERSE:
The King will reply, "I tell you the truth, whatever you did for one of the least of these brothers of mine, you did for me" (Matthew 25:40).

TODAY'S FOCUS:
When you help people in need, you are ultimately giving to Christ Himself. Such compassion will be greatly rewarded.

READ:
Pray for kindness.

A. The Son of Man, the King, will someday judge all people. Describe the kind of people to whom He will give the kingdom.

B. Why is a compassionate, righteous person so blessed?

C. Instead of being selfish and self-centered, I:

NEED:
Thank God for the inheritance He will give you.
    My greatest need today is:

    God answered my prayers today _____
(date) in this way:

DEED:
Pray for compassion for people.
    Lord Jesus, bring some needy person into
my life today that I may:

▲

APPLICATION:
List ways you can practically be kind and compassionate to people around you who are hurting. How can you help them socially, emotionally, physically, financially, spiritually?

LEAD BY SERVING

Mark 10:17–45

▼

KEY VERSES:
Whoever wants to become great among you must be your servant, and whoever wants to be first must be slave of all. For even the Son of Man did not come to be served, but to serve, and to give his life as a ransom for many (Mark 10:43–45).

TODAY'S FOCUS:
Jesus modeled a life of serving rather than seeking personal benefits. As His follower, you are called to do the same. Contrary to popular opinion, the way to lead is by serving others.

READ:
Pray for discernment to understand Christ's words.

A. What are the characteristics of a follower of Christ?

B. Why become a servant?

C. Instead of trying to be first, I will:

NEED:
Thank Christ for serving us.
   My greatest need today is:

   God answered my prayers today _____
(date) in this way:

DEED:
Pray for the humility to serve others.
   Lord, teach me to be like You and to serve
others by:

▲

APPLICATION:
List the hindrances you face in genuinely serving other people. How can you conquer them to
become a servant-leader?

SEEK GODLY VALUES

Luke 12:13–34

▼

KEY VERSES:

Do not set your heart on what you will eat or drink; do not worry about it. For the pagan world runs after all such things, and your Father knows that you need them. But seek his kingdom, and these things will be given to you as well (Luke 12:29–31).

TODAY'S FOCUS:

What you treasure reveals your value system. If you spend your time accumulating things here on earth, to the exclusion of making spiritual investments, your soul will end up bankrupt. God's provisions are given to those who treasure His values.

READ:

Pray for insight into your values.

A. What was wrong with the rich man's attitudes?

B. Why is it foolish to worry?

C. I will seek God's kingdom because:

NEED:
Thank God for meeting your needs each day.
My greatest need today is:

God answered my prayers today _____ (date) in this way:

DEED:
Pray for the ability to overcome greed and worry.
Father, I desire to be a more giving person. Guide me to:

▲

APPLICATION:
Write out a plan for how you will minimize greed and worry. Start with making a budget to handle your finances so you can give generously to God.

NUMBER YOUR DAYS

Psalm 90:1–17

▼

KEY VERSE:
Teach us to number our days aright, that we may gain a heart of wisdom (Psalm 90:12).

TODAY'S FOCUS:
In light of eternity, your life is short. Understanding God's eternal strength and unfailing love will make your days full of gladness. The wise person is the one who makes the most of each day with God's perspective in mind.

READ:
Pray for a heart of wisdom.

A. List the characteristics of the Lord and you.

God	Me

B. How can you handle the troubles and sorrows of life?

C. Teach me, Lord, to:

NEED:
Thank God for gladness in the midst of afflic-
tion.

My greatest need today is:

God answered my prayers today _____
(date) in this way:

DEED:
Pray that you can help someone realize God's
perspective of life.

Ideas I want to convey:

▲

APPLICATION:
Read Proverbs 14. Write a description of a wise
person.

STOP COMPLAINING ABOUT YOUR WEAKNESSES

Exodus 4:1–17

▼

KEY VERSE:
Now go; I will help you speak and will teach you what to say (Exodus 4:12).

TODAY'S FOCUS:
It's easy to complain and feel inadequate. Instead of focusing on what you don't have, focus today on who God is and His resources.

READ:
Pray that you will be obedient.

A. God asked Moses to go to Egypt to lead His people out of bondage and into the Promised Land. What did Moses think about Himself?

B. What did God do to give Moses courage?

C. I will obey God's commands because:

NEED:
Thank God for His resources He gives to you.
My greatest need today is:

God answered my prayers today _____
(date) in this way:

DEED:
Pray for courage to help needy people.
Lord, give me your strength to:

▲

APPLICATION:
Write down the verses that help you see God's
strength in your areas of weaknesses. Review
the verses when you feel like quitting. Read
Galatians 6:7–10.

LEARN TO BE TRULY HAPPY

Matthew 5:1–16

▼

KEY VERSES:

Blessed are those who hunger and thirst for righteousness, for they will be filled. Blessed are the merciful, for they will be shown mercy. Blessed are the pure in heart, for they will see God (Matthew 5:6–8).

TODAY'S FOCUS:

The source of personal happiness is no mystery. God blesses people who incorporate His perspectives into their attitudes and actions.

READ:

Pray for a pure heart.

A. The word *blessed* means happy. What are the characteristics of truly happy people?

B. Regardless of your circumstances, what should you do?

C. Because I want to be happy, I will:

NEED:
Thank God for His precious promises.
My greatest need today is:

God answered my prayers today _____
(date) in this way:

DEED:
Pray that your light may shine brightly.
Lord, let my confidence in You shine forth
so that:

▲

APPLICATION:
Examine yourself in light of the qualities that
Christ commends. Which of these qualities are
present in your life? Which do you need to improve?

RENEW YOUR MIND

Romans 12:1–21

▼

KEY VERSES:
I urge you, brothers, in view of God's mercy, to
offer your bodies as living sacrifices, holy and
pleasing to God—this is your spiritual act of
worship. Do not conform any longer to the pat-
tern of this world, but be transformed by the
renewing of your mind. Then you will be able to
test and approve what God's will is—his good,
pleasing and perfect will (Romans 12:1–2).

TODAY'S FOCUS:
Renewing your mind is the only way to have a
truly biblical perspective of living. Pass your
thoughts through the filter of God's eternal
Word.

READ:
Pray for knowledge of your spiritual gifts.

A. God has given one or more spiritual gifts to each Christian. What attitudes are important for you to have about yourself and your gifts?

B. No matter what gifts you possess, how should you treat other people?

C. My attitudes and actions need to be transformed. This is what I will change:

NEED:
Thank God for His good and perfect will.
    My greatest need today is:

    God answered my prayers today _____
(date) in this way:

DEED:
Pray for devotion to others.
    Lord, use my gifts to:

▲

APPLICATION:
List the spiritual gifts in Romans 12. Which do
you have? What should you do with them?

BUILD UP THE BODY OF CHRIST

Ephesians 4:1–16

▼

KEY VERSES:

Speaking the truth in love, we will in all things grow up into him who is the Head, that is, Christ. From him the whole body, joined and held together by every supporting ligament, grows and builds itself up in love, as each part does its work (Ephesians 4:15–16).

TODAY'S FOCUS:

Christ is the head of the Body of believers. He wants each individual part to do its work well so we will all become united and mature. You are important in God's plan.

READ:

Pray to develop a mature faith.

A. What are the spiritual gifts mentioned here?

B. What are the purposes of the different gifts?

C. Using what God has given me, I will:

NEED:
Thank God for godly leaders and servants.
   My greatest need today is:

   God answered my prayers today _____ (date) in this way:

DEED:
Pray that you will use your gifts to build the Body of Christ.
   O Christ, I want to grow up in every aspect of my life and to:

▲

APPLICATION:
Read 1 Peter 4:7-11 and reread Ephesians 4:11-13. Write down each of the spiritual gifts mentioned in these passages and add them to the list from Romans 12. Evaluate again which ones you have.

KNOW YOUR PLACE IN THE BODY

1 Corinthians 12:4–31

▼

KEY VERSES:
But in fact God has arranged the parts in the body, every one of them, just as he wanted them to be. If they were all one part, where would the body be? As it is, there are many parts, but one body (1 Corinthians 12:18–20).

TODAY'S FOCUS:
The Holy Spirit has given you gifts so you can be a vital part of the Body of Christ. There are no unimportant parts. You are significant in God's plan.

READ:
Pray to know what your spiritual gifts are.

A. What are the spiritual gifts mentioned here?

B. Each part of a body is important to the whole body. Why are you important to the Body of Christ (all other Christians)?

C. I want to use my spiritual gifts to:

NEED:
Thank God for the gifts He has given you.
    My greatest need today is:

    God answered my prayers today _____
(date) in this way:

DEED:
Pray for a concern for other believers.
    Lord, today use my gifts to:

————▲————

APPLICATION:
Write down each of the spiritual gifts mentioned
in 1 Corinthians 12, adding them to the list from
Romans 12, Ephesians 4, and 1 Peter 4. Which
do you have? How can you more effectively use
your gifts?

LOVE LIKE CHRIST LOVES

1 Corinthians 13:1–13

▼

KEY VERSES:

Love is patient, love is kind. It does not envy, it does not boast, it is not proud. It is not rude, it is not self-seeking, it is not easily angered, it keeps no record of wrongs. Love does not delight in evil but rejoices with the truth. It always protects, always trusts, always hopes, always perserveres (1 Corinthians 13:4–7).

TODAY'S FOCUS:

There are many fine abilities and spiritual gifts you could possess. But the love God describes is the most important quality to possess.

READ:

Pray for love.

A. Regardless of what gifts you have or what circumstances you face, God wants you to be filled with biblical love. List the characteristics of that love:

B. Why is biblical love the greatest thing to possess and express?

C. My response to this passage is:

NEED:
Thank God that His love never fails.
My greatest need today is:

God answered my prayers today _____
(date) in this way:

DEED:
Pray for patience and kindness.
Dear Father, fill me with Your kind of love
so that:

▲

APPLICATION:
Write down verses 4–7. Throughout the passage, substitute "Christ" for the word "love," and "He" for the word "it." How does this help you understand Christ's love for you?

IMPROVE YOURSELF

2 Peter 1:1–11

▼

KEY VERSES:
Therefore, my brothers, be all the more eager to
make your calling and election sure. For if you
do these things, you will never fall, and you will
receive a rich welcome into the eternal kingdom
of our Lord and Savior Jesus Christ (2 Peter
1:10–11).

TODAY'S FOCUS:
Proper self-improvement is based on God's
power and promises. He wants you to become
effective and productive.

READ:
Pray to participate in the divine nature.

DAY 27

A. What has God given you?

B. Because of what you have received, what should you do to improve yourself?

C. These are the things I want to practice:

NEED:
Thank God for His precious promises.
    My greatest need today is:

    God answered my prayers today _____
(date) in this way:

DEED:
Pray for brotherly kindness and love.
    My God and Savior, Jesus Christ, empower
me to:

▲

APPLICATION:
Ask a trusted friend to evaluate your life as to
your strengths and weaknesses. Write out steps
you can take to increase your strengths and
minimize your weaknesses.

REJOICE IN DIFFICULTIES

Philippians 1:12–30

▼

KEY VERSES:
I eagerly expect and hope that I will in no way be ashamed, but will have sufficient courage so that now as always Christ will be exalted in my body, whether by life or by death. For to me, to live is Christ and to die is gain (Philippians 1:20–21).

TODAY'S FOCUS:
The difficulties you face can actually advance the gospel and not impede it. The difference is your attitude.

READ:
Pray that you will exalt Christ.

A. Paul was imprisoned for many years on false charges. What was his attitude about handling difficult circumstances?

B. Even when you are facing difficult circumstances, how can you encourage others?

C. When tough times confront me, I will:

NEED:
Thank God for Christ.
    My greatest need today is:

    God answered my prayers today _____
(date) in this way:

DEED:
Pray for the advancement of the gospel.
    Lord God, give me opportunities to proclaim
Christ.

▲

APPLICATION:
What are the three most troublesome things
confronting you? Pray about them and write out
a specific plan to handle each of them.

LIVE IN HARMONY WITH OTHER PEOPLE

Philippians 2:1–11

▼

KEY VERSE:
Your attitude should be the same as that of
Christ Jesus (Philippians 2:5).

TODAY'S FOCUS:
If you want to develop oneness with people, you
need to be humble and relate to their interests.
Follow Christ, who is the greatest model of
bringing people together.

READ:
Pray for the same attitude Christ had.

A. How does God want you to relate with others?

B. Why is Christ's example of humility so significant?

C. Because I want to be like Christ, I will:

NEED:
Thank Christ for His example of humility.
   My greatest need today is:

   God answered my prayers today _____
(date) in this way:

DEED:
Pray to see other people's interests.
   Lord Jesus Christ, help me become a ser-
vant of others in order to:

▲

APPLICATION:
List the significant people in your life: spouse,
children, close friends, boss, etc. Write out practical ideas as to how you can improve your
relationship with them.

BUILD A PRECIOUS HERITAGE

1 Corinthians 3:1–17

▼

KEY VERSES:

By the grace God has given me, I laid a foundation as an expert builder, and someone else is building on it. But each one should be careful how he builds. For no one can lay any foundation other than the one already laid, which is Jesus Christ (1 Corinthians 3:10–11).

TODAY'S FOCUS:

You have time and many opportunities to build something eternally rewarding on the foundation of Christ. Only what is done for His honor will last.

READ:

Pray for determination to work hard for eternal values.

A. What quality of buildings are people building on Christ? What will happen to them in the future? What are the results of our actions?

B. How does it make you feel when you know you are the following things:
   1. God's fellow worker (verse 9)—

   2. God's field (verse 9)—

   3. God's building (verse 9)—

   4. God's temple (verse 16)—

C. My desire is to build:

NEED:
Thank God you are His temple.
My greatest need today is:

God answered my prayers today _____
(date) in this way:

DEED:
Pray for opportunities to point others to God.
O God, help me to plant and water the seed
of the Word so that:

▲

APPLICATION:
Evaluate your activities. Write down which ones
are producing gold, silver, and costly stones in
the sight of God. Which ones are producing
wood, hay, and straw? What will you change?

FOCUS ON YOUR ULTIMATE FUTURE

Revelation 22:1–21

▼

KEY VERSES:

No longer will there be any curse. The throne of God and of the Lamb will be in the city, and his servants will serve him. They will see his face, and his name will be on their foreheads (Revelation 22:3–4).

TODAY'S FOCUS:

Heaven is greatly desirable. Our lives today are wonderfully affected by the reality of our eternal future!

READ:

Worship God.

A. Describe what God has prepared for you in the future.

B. Why is God's invitation to you so wonderful?

C. The Spirit and the Bride say, "Come." I say:

NEED:
Thank God for heaven.
   My greatest need today is:

   God answered my prayers today _____ (date)
in this way:

DEED:
Pray for the faithfulness to do right.
   Alpha and Omega, help me bring others
into:

———▲———

APPLICATION:
How does knowing the future God has for you
affect your self-image?

LESSONS LEARNED— EVALUATION #2

Now that you've completed the Experiment in *Building a Positive Self-image,* it is important for you to think about what progress you have made. This will help you plan for future development.

Under each area below, circle the number on the progress scale that represents where you are now.

A. My self-image has improved as I have seen God develop me in the following three areas:

1. Something to Change

Starting
Point   Goal

| 1 | 2 | 3 | 4 | 5 |

Explanation of my present progress:

2. Something to Accomplish

Starting
Point   Goal

	1	2	3	4	5	

Explanation of my present progress:

3. Something to Handle:

Starting
Point   Goal

	1	2	3	4	5	

Explanation of my present progress:

B. God has also helped me in other areas.
These are indications of my growth:

C. Here are things that still need to be worked
on:

D. My plan of action to progress in these areas is:

Signed_____

Date_____

IMPROVING YOUR SELF-IMAGE

Building a positive self-image is a life-long process because we are imperfect and live in an imperfect world. Yet, the Lord is committed to developing us every day of our lives.

"Being confident of this, that he who began a good work in you will carry it on to completion until the day of Christ Jesus" (Philippians 1:6).

Continue to study God's Word concerning His working in your life. Determine to live for Him day by day.

"For Christ's love compels us, because we are convinced that one died for all, and therefore all died. And he died for all, that those who live should no longer live for themselves but for him who died for them and was raised again" (2 Corinthians 5:14–15).

Here are some practical steps for you to take to continue to become all that God wants you to be:

1. Believe God that you were made in His image (Genesis 1:26–27).
2. Know you are unconditionally loved by God (John 3:16).
3. Realize you are fully accepted in Christ (Romans 15:7).
4. Believe that Christ lives within you (Galatians 2:20).
5. Trust God that He will never leave you (Hebrews 13:5).
6. Accept God's perspective as the right one (Isaiah 55:8–9).
7. Learn to worship the Lord through difficult times (Psalm 34:1–3).
8. Accept your uniqueness (Psalm 139:1–18).
9. Learn from other people, but don't copy them (John 21.17–23).
10. Discover your spiritual gifts through prayer and experience (2 Timothy 1:5–7).
11. Develop your spiritual gifts through hard work (1 Corinthians 15:9–10).
12. Major in the positive things about you (2 Corinthians 4:7–12).
13. Get additional education if at all possible (Ezra 7:10).
14. Live for Godly values even if it means suffering (2 Timothy 1:11–12).

15. Keep on praying (Luke 18:1–8).
16. Give God time to work. Be patient (Philippians 1:6).
17. Compensate for your weaknesses (2 Corinthians 12:9–10).
18. Use your strengths to build up other people (Ephesians 4:11–13).
19. Seek God's guidance through prayer and Bible study (James 1:5–8).
20. Forgive those who have hurt you (Colossians 3:12–13).
21. Say no to things that pull you down (Genesis 39:2–18).
22. Plan your days and do the most important things first (Ephesians 5:15–17).
23. Refuse to allow discouragement to depress you (2 Corinthians 4:16–18).
24. Be enthusiastic about your job (Colossians 3:23–24).

ADDITIONAL 31-DAY EXPERIMENTS

Now that you have finished a month of studying God's Word and growing closer to God, I hope you will want to continue to spend time alone with the risen Lord. He is the Vine from whom you can receive daily life and nourishment. Intimacy with Him continues and increases as you daily remain in Him.

The *31-Day Experiment* series of books has been designed to help you develop a consistent devotional time with your Heavenly Father. Whether you are a new Christian or have been one for a long time, these *31-Day Experiments* will help you establish an intimate relationship with Christ. You will experience for yourself the joy of discovering God's truth from the Bible.

Although all the Experiment books are designed like the one you have just completed, each book includes different passages and themes for you to study.

At the end of each Experiment is a number of simple Bible study methods or ideas for further growth. These will help you investigate, on your own, more of the truth that the Holy Spirit has given for you to know.

These books are designed to help you get into God's Word, and get God's Word into you:

GROWING CLOSER TO GOD

This is the original *31-Day Experiment* book. It is designed to help you cultivate your knowledge of God by looking at passages in which you can discover more about His ways and perspectives. The process of continuing to know God intimately will affect every area of your life and actually will begin to transform you into the kind of person He wants you to be.

Some of the topics included in the book are:
- God's Plan to Provide for My Needs
- Turning Pain Into Hope
- New Life and New Purpose
- Guidelines for Spiritual and Physical Health
- The Truth About Temptation
- Path to Personal Peace
- The Pleasure of Pleasing God

Two additional simple Bible study methods at the back of the book are explained for you to try. The **first** is a "One-a-Week Bible Topics." You will learn how to find out all that God says on any biblical subject that interests you.

The **second** is "15 Characters for 15 Days." You will be able to investigate the lives of biblical people. To start you off, 15 people are suggested. Each of them can be studied within only 30–45 minutes. The Holy Spirit can teach you some vital lessons through these and other biblical characters.

A PERSONAL EXPERIMENT IN FAITH-BUILDING

God wants your faith to grow. This Experiment book is a biblical study to build your faith in the manner that Christ desires. What ingredients are needed to develop a powerful trust in the Living God? They involve three areas: *knowledge, affirmation*, and *reliance*. You will learn how to increase all of them.

For 16 days you will learn how the Lord Jesus Christ developed the faith of His disciples. Both their successes and failures can teach you to believe the Son of God for greater things in your own life. The rest of the month will be spent observing what the apostle Paul says about building a biblical faith that can unlock for you the supernatural power of Almighty God.

You will learn how to feast upon God's everlasting Word by learning to study "The Great Moments of Faith." Throughout the Bible there are critical events that have shaped the course of history. Who were the people who trusted the Lord against unbelievable odds? Find out how to discover the secrets of their confident faith.

STANDING STRONG IN A GODLESS CULTURE

"Godless" is the word that best characterizes our culture today. People live as though the Lord does not exist. Their days are filled with things to do, and the thought of God seldom enters their minds. Christ is irrelevant to their behavior, decisions, lifestyle and thoughts.

However, the people who know God will be strong and take action. They will shine as lights in this darkened world. God is not looking for superhuman people. He is looking for ordinary people who love Him and will trust His supernatural power.

This Experiment book will prepare you to become strong in the powerful might of the King of Kings. Here are some of the topics you will study during the 31 days of conquering obstacles:

- God Fights for His People
- The Consequences of Obedience
- To Slay a Giant
- Experiencing the Power of God's Word
- Resisting the Pressure to Conform
- The Sustaining Presence of Christ

You also will learn how to do a "Whole Book Study." To study an entire book of the Bible is to capture the heartbeat and powerful message of the divine Author.

Imagine being able to put the entire outline of a biblical book on one sheet of paper. You will start with Jonah. After that, you are encouraged to do a book chart of any other book of the Bible. Finally, there are practical suggestions for using your biblical knowledge to help others build a godly foundation for their lives.

KNOWING GOD BY HIS NAMES

This book took me 13 years to write. I first became interested in the fascinating variety of the names of God when I was a pastor in Indiana.

I started a search in the Bible for God's names. A name to the people in biblical times meant something entirely different from what it does to us today. In our culture a name is given to a child to identify him/her from other people.

But a name in the Bible refers to a particular trait or characteristic about the person. If you understand the meaning of his/her name, you will know something very important about him/her.

Our great Lord has over 200 names! God has so many names because each one puts the spotlight on a particular aspect of His incredibly complex character. No one name could tell you everything there is to know about Him.

This Experiment gives you a different name to study each day. By learning about each name, your understanding of God will increase and your love for our wonderful Lord will grow deeper.

Here are some of the names you will study during the 31 days:

Father
God Almighty
Prince of Peace
LORD (Jehovah)
Most High God

Living God
LORD Who Heals
Son of Man
High Priest
King of Kings
Shepherd

Your prayer life will be transformed. When you have a specific need, you will be able to address God using the name which deals with that situation.

- Anxious? Lean on the Prince of Peace.
- Hurt? Experience comfort from the Heavenly Father.
- Guilty? Find forgiveness from the Lamb of God.
- Insecure and fearful? Look to the Rock.
- Looking for direction? Follow the Shepherd.
- Confused? Come to the Light of the World.

In the back of the book, you will find a list of all the names for God, their characteristics and a key verse to get you started in learning about each name. In addition, there are practical directions to help you unlock the mysteries of God's divine person.

It is an exciting approach to developing a deep intimacy with the Lord of Glory. He wants to reveal Himself to you so that you will respond in obedience, faith, love, and worship.

KNOWING GOD'S HEART, SHARING HIS JOY

Do you understand God's commitment to you? There is a special place for you in His heart and in His eternal plan. Would you like to witness boldly to others about your faith in Christ and your love for Him?

This *31-Day Experiment* will help you learn to effectively share your faith. The book covers these topics:

- Develop the confidence to witness for Christ with courage and joy
- Learn to love the Lord with a clearer understanding of who He really is
- Experience greater appreciation for how God works in your life and in the lives of His people
- See more clearly God's message for everyone
- Develop greater urgency to share God's love with others

- Become equipped to provide the biblical answers for people's needs

As you follow this daily study for a month, you will read about men and women of the Bible who obeyed God and experienced His blessing—and how their godly lives touched those around them.

Discover what God can do in—and through—your life!

ABOUT THE AUTHOR

Dick Purnell is the founder and director of Single Life Resources, a ministry of Campus Crusade for Christ. He is an internationally known speaker and author.

A graduate of Wheaton College, Dick holds a Master of Divinity degree from Trinity Evangelical Divinity School and a master's degree in education (specializing in counseling) from Indiana University.

Dick has authored eight books in the *31-Day Experiment* series. He has also written *Friendship . . . The Basis for Love, Building a Relationship That Lasts* and *Free to Love Again*.

He and his wife Paula have two daughters, and they live in North Carolina.